The Mac
is not a typewriter

The Mac is not a typewriter

A style manual for creating
professional-level type
on your Macintosh

Robin Williams

Peachpit Press
Berkeley • California

Peachpit Press

2414 Sixth Street

Berkeley · California · 94710

510.548-4393

800.283.9444

510.548.5991 fax

Library of Congress Cataloging-in-Publication Data
Williams, Robin
The Mac is not a typewriter
        Includes index
        1. Desktop publishing—Style manuals.
2. Macintosh (Computer)—Programming.   I. Title.
Z286.D47W538   1990
686.2'2544536–dc20   90–7508 CIP

ISBN 0-938151-31-2

Sixteenth Printing
Printed and bound in the United States of America

*To the memory of William Strunk, Jr.,
whose writings and philosophy taught me
to "make definite assertions."*

Remember, the music is not in the piano.
　　　　　　—Clement Mok, *Clement Mok Designs*

Contents.

Read me first.

It has long been an axiom of mine that the little things are infinitely the most important.

Sir Arthur Conan Doyle, 1925

This phenomenon of desktop publishing is certainly incredible. Never before has professional-level type been available so readily and easily and, best of all, inexpensively—even the smallest business or the most harried college student can create high-quality pages, from annual reports to a letter for Mom to theses papers to visual presentations.

Thousands of us are circumventing the professional typesetters and creating this type ourselves, assuming that because this machine has a keyboard it works like a typewriter. Wrong. Professional typesetters know things we don't. This book does not pretend to be a treatise on design or typography or desktop publishing—there are many excellent books available in those areas. Rather, the purpose of this book is to let you in on some of the secrets that have been used for centuries to make type pleasing, beautiful, readable, legible, and artistic—secrets we just weren't taught in Typing 1A.

Many of the concepts presented in this book are subtle, yes—but they add up to a professional look. Perhaps most people couldn't put a finger on exactly what *gives* it that look, but everyone is aware of it. If we are taking type out of the hands of professionals, then we must upgrade *our* awareness of what makes their work *look* professional. It's just a matter of raising our consciousness, of looking closer at our printed pages with a bit more critical eye.

And of forgetting the rules our typing teachers taught us. **The Mac is not a typewriter.** The type we are using is not mono-spaced, mono-weight, mono-sized, mono-boring; it's capable of being the highest quality. And, as Mies van der Rohe said, "God is in the details."

I strongly feel it is our obligation—every one of us who uses the computer to create text on a page—to uphold the highest possible level of typographic quality in this changing world.

One space between sentences.

Use only one space after periods, colons, exclamation points, question marks, quotation marks—any punctuation that separates two sentences.

What? you say! Yes—for years you've been told to hit two spaces after periods, and on a typewriter you should. But this is no typewriter.

On a typewriter, all the characters are **monospaced;** that is, they each take up the same amount of space—the letter **i** takes up as much space as the letter **m.** Because they are monospaced, you need to type two spaces after periods to separate one sentence from the next. But . . .

On a Macintosh (unless you're using the fonts Monaco or Courier, which are monospaced just like a typewriter and what would you want to use those for anyway) the characters are **proportional;** that is, they each take up a proportional amount of space—the letter **i** takes up about one-fifth the space of the letter **m.** So you no longer need extra spaces to separate the sentences. Take a careful look at these two examples:

```
Notice in this paragraph how the letters
line up in columns, one under the other,
just as on your typewriter.  This is
because each character takes up the same
amount of space.  This monospacing is
what makes it necessary to use two
spaces to separate sentences.
```

This paragraph, however, uses a font with *proportional* spacing. Each character takes up a proportional amount of the space available. Thus the single space between sentences is enough to visually separate them, and two spaces creates a disturbing gap.

Of course, this one-space rule applies just as well to the spacing after colons, semi-colons, question marks, quotation marks, exclamation points, or any other punctuation you can think of. Yes, this is a difficult habit to break, but it must be done.

Take a look at any magazine or book on your shelf—you will never find two spaces between sentences (the only exception will be publications or advertisements produced on the Mac by someone who was still following typewriter rules).

Quotation marks.

Use real quotation marks—never those grotesque generic marks that actually symbolize inch or foot marks: use " and " — not " and ".

Of course, on a typewriter when you wanted quotation marks you used the typewriter quote marks, the ones that otherwise one would think are inch marks (") and foot marks ('). Those symbols are never found, though, as quotation marks in a book, magazine, ad, poster, etc., simply because that is not what they are.

Fortunately, the Mac thoughtfully provides us with real quotation marks. Unfortunately, they're tucked away on one of those invisible keyboards that you can only see with the desk accessory Key Caps (see page 21 for more info on Key Caps). It takes an extra split second to access them, but you get used to it. The subtle, added professionalism they give your work is very well worth the effort, even on the ImageWriter. This is where they are hidden:

Opening double quote:	"	Option [
Closing double quote:	"	Option Shift [
Opening single quote:	'	Option]
Closing single quote:	'	Option Shift]

Do you see the pattern? When you are typing, instead of pressing the revolting " key, hold down the Option and/or Shift keys while you press the opening or closing bracket (near the Return key). You may even want to put a piece of tape on those bracket keys and draw in the proper quote marks to remind you exactly where they are.

Some software applications will convert the typewriter quotes to the real quotes for you automatically, but it is sensible to get accustomed to placing them yourself. They are also available at your Desktop when you're naming files, as well as in the Save As... dialog boxes, in paint programs, database and spreadsheet programs—just any-where you can type. There's no excuse for not using them. *Typewriter quotation marks are the single most visible sign of unprofessional type.*

Punctuation used with quote marks

There often seems to be confusion about where the quotation marks belong when there is punctuation involved. These are the guidelines:

- Commas and periods are **always** placed **inside** the quotation marks. Always. Really.

- Colons and semicolons go **outside** the quotation marks.

- Question marks and exclamation points go **in or out,** depending on whether they belong to the material inside the quote or not. Logically, if they *belong* to the quoted material, they go *inside* the quote marks, and vice versa.

- If more than one paragraph is quoted, the double quote is placed at the beginning of each paragraph, but only at the end of the last one. What an interesting convention.

postrophes.

Use real apostrophes, not the foot marks: ' not '.

This is actually exactly the same as the previous chapter, but it's set off separately because it is so important and often people don't connect quotation marks with apostrophes. But the apostrophe is nothing more than the single closing quotation mark.

Repeated from the previous page:

Apostrophe: **'** Option Shift]

Apostrophe rules

As an aside, people often are confused about where the apostrophe belongs. There are a couple of rules that work very well:

For possessives: Turn the phrase around. The apostrophe will be placed after whatever word you end up with.

For example, in the phrase **the boys' camp,** to know where to place the apostrophe say to yourself, "The camp belongs to the **boys.**"

The phrase **the boy's camp** says "The camp belongs to the **boy.**"

Another example: **the women's room;** "The room belongs to the **women.**"

> **The big exception to this is "its."** "Its" used as a possessive *never* has an apostrophe!!! The word **it** only has an apostrophe as a contraction—"it's" always means "it is" or "it has." **Always.**
>
> It may be easier to remember if you recall that **yours, hers,** and **his** don't use apostrophes—and neither should **its.**

■

For contractions: The apostrophe replaces the missing letter.

For example: **you're** always means **you are;** the apostrophe is replacing the **a** from **are.** That's an easy way to distinguish it from **your** as in **your** house and to make sure you *don't* say: Your going to the store.

As previously noted, **it's** means "it is"; the apostrophe is indicating where the **i** is left out. **Don't** means "do not"; the apostrophe is indicating where the **o** is left out.

For omission of letters: In a phrase such as **Rock 'n' Roll**, there should be an apostrophe *before and after* the **n,** because the **a** and the **d** are both left out. And don't turn the first apostrophe around—just because it appears in *front* of the letter does not mean you need to use the opposite single quote. An apostrophe is still the appropriate mark (*not* **'n'**).

In a phrase such as **House o' Fashion**, the apostrophe takes the place of the **f.** There is no earthly reason for an apostrophe to be set *before* the **o.**

In a phrase such as **Gone Fishin'** the same pattern is followed—the **g** is missing.

In a date when part of the year is left out, an apostrophe needs to indicate the missing year. **In the 80s** would mean the temperature; **In the '80s** would mean the decade. (Notice there is no apostrophe before the **s**! Why would there be? It is not possessive, nor is it a contraction—it is simply a plural.)

Dashes.

Never use two hyphens instead of a dash.
Use hyphens, en dashes, and em dashes appropriately.

Everyone knows what a hyphen is—that tiny little dash that belongs in some words, like mother-in-law, or in phone numbers. It's also used to break a word at the end of a line, of course.

On a typewriter, we were taught to use a double hyphen to indicate a dash, like so: -- . We were taught that because typewriters didn't have a real dash, as the professional typesetters have. With the Mac, we no longer need to use the double hyphen—we have an **em dash,** which is a long dash, such as you see in this sentence. We also have an **en dash,** which is a little shorter than the em dash.

Hyphen -
A hyphen is strictly for hyphenating words or line breaks. Your punctuation style manual goes into great detail about when to use a hyphen; there doesn't seem to be a great deal of confusion surrounding that issue. We all know where to find it—on the upper right of the keyboard, next to the equal sign.

En dash –
An en dash is called an en dash because it's approximately the width of a capital letter N in that particular font and size. It is used between words **indicating a duration,** such as hourly time or months or years. Use it where you might otherwise use the word "to." The en dash can be used with a thin space on either side of it, if you want a little room, but don't use a full space. Here are a few examples of places to use the en dash. Notice that, really, these are *not* hyphenated words, and a plain hyphen is not the logical character to use.

October – December

7:30 – 9:45 A.M.

3 – 5 years of age

■

The en dash is also used when you have a compound adjective and one of the elements is made of two words or a hyphenated word, such as:

San Francisco–Chicago flight
pre–Vietnam war period
high-class–high-energy lifestyle

Em dash —

The **em dash** is twice as long as the en dash—it's about the size of a capital letter M. This dash is often used in a manner similar to a colon or parentheses, or it indicates an abrupt change in thought, or it's used in a spot where a period is too strong and a comma is too weak (check your punctuation style manual for the exact use of the dash, if you're unsure). Our equivalent on the typewriter was the double hyphen, but now we have a real em dash.

Since you were properly taught, of course, you know that the double hyphen is not supposed to have a space on either side of it—neither is the em dash, as you can see right here in this sentence. There are six other examples of the em dash in this chapter.

OK—so where do you find those characters?

- **hyphen**   Next to the zero at the top right of the keyboard

– **en dash**   Option Hyphen
(hold the Option key down while pressing the hyphen)

— **em dash**   Option Shift Hyphen
(hold the Option *and* Shift keys down while pressing the hyphen)

City-named fonts and the dashes

Please read the chapter on Fonts (p. 35) to understand the difference between city-named fonts and those without city names. Regarding en and em dashes, some city-named fonts have them switched; that is, fonts like Geneva or New York access the en dash with Option Shift Hyphen and the em dash with Option Hyphen.

Special characters.

Take advantage of the special characters available.

Consistent with the purpose of letting us create professional-level type right at our desktop, the Mac provides us with such marks as ®, ™, ¢, etc., which are the particular topic of this chapter, as well as such luxuries as accent marks that can be placed right over the letter they belong to (dealt with in the following chapter), and real quotation marks and apostrophes (see pages 15 and 17).

Key Caps

If you haven't looked at your desk accessory Key Caps, you should. It's under the Apple menu on the far left. When you pull down Key Caps, you see a layout of the keyboard (provided your keyboard layout icon is loaded into your System Folder). In the upper right of the menu bar you'll see a new menu item: **Key Caps.** Under that item is a list of the fonts you have on your System. Choose the font you'd like to see on the layout (LaserWriter fonts have more characters available).

What you initially see are the same keys you see on your keyboard in front of you, under your fingers. If you hold down the Shift key, on the Key Caps layout you'll see the Shift key depressed and a second key layout—all the capital letters and the Shift-characters. You knew all about those two layouts already.

There are actually two more keyboard layouts available to you. Many of the characters are consistent in every font; some fonts may have more alternates available than others. Press the Option key down— now you see all the Option-characters available in that particular font. The accent marks are all hidden in here, as well as symbols like ¢, ¡, ÷, £, or 🐇. If you hold the Option and the Shift keys down, you see another set of symbols (can you find the real apostrophe?). Try selecting different fonts from the Key Caps menu and viewing all the special characters belonging to the other fonts.

To use these characters in your document, follow these steps:

1. If you don't know exactly which keys will give you the desired mark, choose Key Caps from the Apple menu (if you already know which keys because you looked it up in Appendix B at the back of this book, then skip to step #6).

2. From the new menu item, Key Caps, choose the name of a font. You will see a keyboard layout for that font.

3. Find the character you want to use; if you don't see it on the screen immediately, press the Shift key, the Option key, or the Shift and Option keys together.

4. Notice where the character appears on the screen keyboard; find that key on the keyboard under your fingers.

5. Once you know which keys you need to create that character, remember them and go back to your document.

6. Set the insertion point where you want the new character to appear.

7. If the character is in a font that is different from the one you are currently using, then choose that font from your menu—otherwise, never mind.

8. Press the appropriate keys; e.g., in the font Times, hold down the Option key and press J to get this mark: Δ.

9. If that character came from a different font than you were using in your document, you will have to choose your original font again from the menu, as the insertion point continues typing in whatever character is directly to its left, even if that character is a blank space.

   ▪ To circumvent that situation, just press the Option/Shift/character keys in whatever font you are using—you will come up with some strange character.

   ▪ When you are done with the sentence, come back to that character, select it, and change it to the font you need.

- If you find you need it regularly—a Zapf Dingbats checkbox at the beginning of each paragraph, for example—then type in the key combination along with typing the rest of the document, even though it creates a strange character; change the first one to Zapf Dingbats; copy it; select the rest one at a time; replace them by pasting in the copied character. Or use the search-and-replace feature, if you have one.

Superscript and Subscript

Don't forget about the superscript and subscript possibilities you have. Most applications offer this in the menu that deals with type.

- To create a superscript such as the **rd** in **3rd**, simply do this: type **3rd**; select the **rd** and choose "superscript."
- To create a subscript such as the **2** in **H_2O**, simply do this: type **H2O**; select the **2** and choose "subscript."

If your application allows you to use a keyboard command shortcut for super- and subscripts, then use that shortcut *before* you type the character; then *after* you type it, *use the same keyboard shortcut* to return to normal type. For instance, if the keyboard shortcut is Command Shift **+** for superscript, then you could type the following sequence to get **3rd place**:

type **3**	then press Command Shift **+**
type **rd**	then press Command Shift **+**
hit the *Spacebar*	then type **place**

Fractions

Ever wonder where the fractions are? There aren't any. Generally speaking, anyway—some of the newer fonts have a few of the most common. If you're writing a math book, you would probably want to invest in a specialized font that carries them all. But for occasional use, try this trick:

- Type the whole number and the fraction with no space between, like so: **21/2** (use the fraction bar instead of the slash: Shift Option !).

- Select the **1** and make it a superscript (you'll usually find super- and subscript in the type style menu; every program has them somewhere);

- Select the **2** and change its size to about half the point size of the original text.

- It'll look like this: **2½.** Isn't that pretty?

  Kerning (page 33) can help adjust the numbers around the fraction bar.

A list for you

Below is a list of the commonly-used special characters in general typing. To create any of these, hold down the Shift and/or Option key while you press the letter for that character. See the following chapter for creating accent marks.

"   Option   [opening double quote

"   Option   Shift   [closing double quote

'   Option   ]   opening single quote

'   Option   Shift   ]   closing single quote; apostrophe

–   Option   hyphen   en dash

—   Option   Shift   hyphen   em dash

…   Option   ;   ellipsis   (this character can't be separated at the end of a line as three periods can)

•   Option   8   bullet (easy to remember as it's the asterisk key)

fi   Option   Shift   5   ligature of f and i

fl   Option   Shift   6   ligature of f and l

©   Option   g

™   Option   2

®   Option   r

°   Option   Shift   8   degree symbol (e.g., 102°F)

¢   Option $

/   Option   Shift   !   fraction bar (this doesn't descend below the line as the slash does)

¡   Option   1

¿   Option   Shift   ?

£   Option   3

ç   Option   c

Ç   Option   Shift   c

Accent marks.

Where an accent mark is appropriate, use it.

The accent marks are a little sneakier than the special characters—easy, but sneaky. If you've ever tried to use the tilde key to type the word piñata with the tilde over the n, you've noticed that it doesn't work—you get pin~ata. That doesn't look very intelligent.

This is the trick: The accent marks are all hidden on the Option keyboard. First find out (either from this chart, the chart at the end of the book, or in your Key Caps; see page 21) which letter is hiding the accent mark; typically it's the character with which the accent mark is most likely to be used.

To type an accent over a letter in your document, first hold down the Option key and hit the accent character; nothing will happen. That's good! Now, type the character you want *under* that accent mark; they will then appear together.

For example, to type **résumé**:

- Pull down Key Caps and notice on the layout that you get the accent mark ´ with the combination of the Option key and the letter **e**. Close Key Caps (**or** you could just look up the key combination on the chart).
- Type **r**.
- Now hold down the Option key and press the letter **e**; nothing will happen.
- Now, *without* holding down the Option key, type the letter **e**; you will get **é**.
- Repeat the sequence when you get to the last **e**.

A list of the accent marks and where to find them is on the next page, as well as in Appendix B at the end of the book.

This is where you'll find the accent marks:

ʹ   Option e

ˋ   Option ~   (upper left or next to the spacebar)

¨   Option u

~ Option n

^ Option i

This accent mark is only found on the letter c, so it just comes along with the letter; there is no need to press twice:

ç   Option c

Ç   Option Shift c

Underlining.

Don't underline. Underlining is for typewriters; italic is for professional text.

Have you ever seen a word underlined in a magazine or a book? Most likely not. That's because typesetters are able to *italicize* words for emphasis or for proper convention (such as book titles, periodicals, operas, symphonies).

On a typewriter, of course, we had no way to italicize. So we were taught to underline words for emphasis, or to underline those items just mentioned—books, periodicals, etc. Since we are upgrading the quality of our type, we should follow the professional standard of italicizing those items that should be italicized.

Underlining in general should be avoided—the underline tends to be heavy, is too close to the type, and bumps into the "descenders" of the letters (those parts that hang below the line, as in the letters g, j, p, q, and y).

If you want to emphasize a word or two, you have other options also. Try **bold type,** larger type, **or a different font.**

Simply setting it apart from the rest of the copy can call extra attention to a bit of text.

This doesn't mean you should never have any sort of underline with text—just don't use the underline style that appears on the menu. If you really do want the *look* of an underline, use a drawn line (called a "rule" in typesetter's jargon). Most word processors and all page layout, paint, and draw programs have some way for you to draw a line under a word or headline. When you draw a line, you can place it where you want and make it as thick or thin or long as you want. You can avoid making the line bump into the descenders. The drawn line also tends to look smoother than the underline because it is one long line, not a series of short lines hooked together.

<u>This is an underlined phrase.</u>

This phrase has a rule drawn under it.

This phrase has an *italic* word.

Capitals.

Very rarely (almost never) use all capital letters.

On a typewriter, our only way to make a headline stand out was to type it in all caps, or maybe underline it. Now, of course, we can make the text larger, or bold, or shadowed, or outlined, or underlined, or any gross combination of all those. We no longer need to rely on all caps to make something noticeable. And we shouldn't.

Many studies have shown that all caps are much harder to read. We recognize words not only by their letter groups, but also by their shapes, sometimes called the "coastline." Take a look at these words and their shapes:

When these words are all caps, can you tell their shapes apart?

When a word is all caps, we have to read it letter by letter, rather than by recognizing groups of letters. Try reading this block of text set in all caps; be conscious of how much slower than usual you read it and how tiring it is on your eyes.

> WEN YOU'RE A MARRIED MAN, SAMIVEL, YOU'LL UNDERSTAND A GOOD MANY THINGS AS YOU DON'T UNDERSTAND NOW; BUT VETHER IT'S WORTH WHILE GOIN' THROUGH SO MUCH TO LEARN SO LITTLE, AS THE CHARITY-BOY SAID VEN HE GOT TO THE END OF THE ALPHABET, IS A MATTER O' TASTE.
>
> Charles Dickens, *Pickwick Papers*

Setting a *strange-looking* font in all caps is particularly bad news, or setting italic or calligraphy or an italic-outlined-bold-shadowed-underlined face in reverse on a patterned background—aack! Take a look at how this font in all caps becomes almost impossible to read:

𝔐𝔄𝔆𝔍𝔑𝔗𝔒𝔖𝔥 𝔐𝔄𝔇𝔑𝔈𝔖𝔖   (12 point, TypoUpright regular)

All caps also takes up a lot more space. With lowercase letters, you can make the type size bigger and bolder in the same amount of space, which will be more efficient and more effective.

Macintosh Madness   (14 point, Futura bold)

Occasionally you may have some very good reason to use all caps in a very short block of text or in a heading. Sometimes the particular look you want on the page can only be created with all caps. When you do that, just be aware of the inherent problems; recognize that you're making a choice between a design solution and the legibility/ readability of the piece. Be able to justify the choice.

A little puzzle

Here is a fun little teaser to impress upon you how much we depend on word shapes to read. On the following lines are two well-known proverbs. The letters are indicated only by black rectangles the size of each letter. Can you read the sentences? How quickly would you be able to read them if they were set this way in all caps?

1. ▌▪▪▌▐▪▌ ▪▐▪▪▪ ▌▪▐▌▪▪▪
   ▪▪ ▪▪▪▌.

2. ▌▪▪ ▪▪▪ ▐▪▪▌ ▪ ▐▪▪▪▪ ▐▪
   ▪▪▐▪▪, ▐▪▌ ▌▪▪ ▪▪▪'▐ ▪▪▐▪
   ▐▪▪ ▐▪▐▪▌.

Kerning.

Adjust the space between letters according to your sensitive visual perception.

One of the most important things a professional typesetter does for a client is **kern** the type. **Kerning** is the process of removing small units of space between letters in order to create *visually-consistent letterspacing;* the larger the letters, the more critical it is to adjust their spacing. Awkward letterspacing not only looks naïve and unprofessional, it can disrupt the communication of the words. Look carefully at these two examples (try squinting):

WASHINGTON unkerned

WASHINGTON kerned

The secret of kerning is that *it is totally dependent on your eye, not on the machine*. In the first example, each letter has mechanically the same amount of space on either side of it. Some spaces *appear* to be larger because of the shape of the letter—angled or rounded. In the second example, the computer application was set to adjust, or kern, the letters, and it did a fairly good job, but the letters still needed some manual adjusting. *Type needs a human eye for the fine tuning.*

Take a look at the square and circle below—which appears to be larger?

  Actually, they are both exactly the same size from edge to edge. The circle *appears* to be smaller because of all the white space surrounding it. It is this fact that creates the need to manually and visually letterspace/kern type— each character presents a different visual impression on the page, and reacts with the other letters according to their particular combinations of dark and light space. These impressions can be broken down into a few generalized combinations:

HL Characters with verticals next to each other need the most amount of space; this can often be used as a guideline with which to keep the spacing consistent.

HO A vertical next to a curve needs less space.

OC A curve next to a curve needs very little space.

OT A curve can actually overlap into the white space under or above the bar or stem of a character, and vice versa.

AT The closest kerning is done where both letters have a great deal of white space around them.

Remember, the point is to keep the spacing visually consistent—there should visually *appear* to be the same amount of space between all the letters. It's not critical how much—it's critical that whatever it is be consistent. You can usually focus better on that white space if you look at the text with your eyes squinted.

Kerning is not possible in all applications; typically you'll find it in page layout programs or in applications where text manipulation is a primary feature. You won't usually find it possible to control the kerning in a word processor.

In those applications where it *is* possible, each character and space is broken down into little sections, called *units;* 48 units per character is a common breakdown. Using the kerning function, it is possible to take out one of those units at a time between letters, allowing for very precise positioning. Check the manual for the particular method for kerning in your application.

Fonts.

*Use bitmapped fonts on low-resolution printers
and PostScript fonts on PostScript printers.*

At the time of this printing, the font scene is muddled with differing technologies, and it will take a while for the dust to settle. If you are working exclusively with System 7 and TrueType, this chapter is not so relevant. If you are using System 6, this chapter is still pertinent to the look of your documents.

You may have noticed that the fonts on your list are divided into two categories: those with city names and those without city names.

Almost any font with a city name is a bitmapped font, designed to be readable at the lower resolution of the computer screen and of QuickDraw printers, such as the ImageWriter. PostScript laser printers, such as the Apple LaserWriter, cannot understand bitmapped fonts! All a PostScript printer can do for city-named fonts is recreate what you have on the screen—the type will still be bitmapped and lumpy. You'll get a little dialog box while printing to a laser printer telling you it's creating a bitmapped font.

The exceptions to this are the city-named fonts that are designed to emulate the traditional fonts—they create a different problem:

Times ....New York

Helvetica ....Geneva

Courier ....Monaco

Times is a traditional font and is installed directly in most laser printers; New York, which we can associate with The Times, is the bitmapped version of Times, designed to meet the needs of the lower resolution of the screen and QuickDraw printers.

Helvetica, another traditional font installed in most laser printers, is named after Switzerland (Confederatio Helvetia), the country where the typeface was created; Geneva, which we can associate with Switzerland, is the bitmapped version of Helvetica.

Courier, which looks like monospaced typewriter type (and why anyone would want to use a laser printer to make their work look like a typewriter is a mystery to me), has a bitmapped equivalent called Monaco.

The point of all this is that if you use one of those three bitmapped fonts just named (New York, Geneva, or Monaco) on a laser printer, many applications will use what appear to be their equivalents (they will *substitute* fonts); your type will not be bitmapped, but will look similar to the traditional font. What you will notice, though, are disturbing spaces between the words; your tabs won't line up properly; your underlining will show little gaps between the dashes; your formatting may be off; your work won't always print exactly as you have it on your screen. Here are some examples:

- This is 10 point New York printed on the LaserWriter with no font substitution. Notice the bitmapped look.

- This is 10 point New York printed on the LaserWriter with automatic font substitution. The resolution is better, but notice the disgusting word spacing.

- This is 10 point Times printed on the LaserWriter. It doesn't need font substitution. It looks great.

If you're doing a lot of word processing, it's easier to read city-named fonts on the screen. If you're going to be printing your work on a low resolution printer, city-named fonts will be more readable. If you are just going to *proof* your work on, say, an ImageWriter, it would be sensible to input all your text in something like Geneva or New York and then format it into the PostScript fonts for the final printouts on the laser printer.

All PostScript fonts look just lovely on high-end printers such as the Linotronic, and the bitmapped fonts look even more awful.

Tabs & Indents.

Use those tabs and first-line indents regularly.
Never use the space bar to align text.

Too many people try to use the spacebar to line up words or numbers. That method works on a typewriter because every letter takes up the same amount of space, so five spaces is always five spaces. This is not true on a Mac. If you want things to align, you *must* use tabs.

The first-line indent marker is often overlooked. What a wonderful invention! Remember on a typewriter when you wanted to indent your paragraphs? You would set a tab for five spaces in from the left margin, and at the end of a paragraph hit the carriage return, hit the tab key, then begin typing again. Well, the first-line indent does all of that for you: when you set the indentation you want, every time you hit the Return key (only at the end of a *paragraph*, remember, not the end of every line because the type *word wraps* at the right margin), the first line of your next paragraph will automatically indent. Like so:

> There is a tide in the affairs of men, which, taken at the flood, leads on to fortune; omitted, all the voyage of their life is bound in shallows and in miseries.
>
> On such a full sea are we now afloat; and we must take the current when it serves, or lose our ventures.
> —*William Shakespeare*

— These indentations were set with a first-line indent, *not* a tab.

You can do just the opposite to create a hanging paragraph, like so:

> The poor world is almost six thousand years old, and in all this time there was not any man died in his own person, *videlicet*, in a love-cause.
> …But these are all lies: men have died from time to time and worms have eaten them, but not for love.

— These indentations were also set using the first-line indent; the first line was set to the *left* of the margin marker.

Before explaining exactly how to create these interesting arrangements, let's get straight what all the little marks in the rulers are for. Your ruler may not look exactly like the one shown, but it will work in a similar fashion.

Generally in the application there is some sort of Page Setup command in the File menu where you set up the outer margins of your page. Then what you see as zero on your ruler is actually *zero inches in from the left of that margin* you specified in Page Setup.

At the zero marker you'll find a triangle pointing to the right; at the other end, again correlating with the margin in Page Setup, you'll see a triangle pointing to the left. These are the left and right margins—your type will begin at the left margin and continue to the right margin. When text reaches the right margin, it *automatically word-wraps* and takes itself to the next line, back to the left margin, without your having to hit a Return.

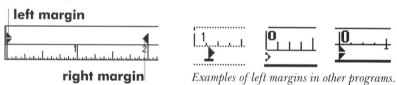

Examples of left margins in other programs.

You may have noticed that the left margin marker is usually made of two parts, and each part can travel separately. One part of the marker is actually *not* the left margin—it is the **first-line indent.** As mentioned on the previous page, this is the marker that eliminates the need to hit the Tab key for paragraph indentations.

> **Every time you press the Return key the text will return to wherever you set *the first-line indent*. When the text reaches the right margin, it will word wrap and will line up at the point where you set the *left margin marker*.** To set the first-line indent, simply press on it and drag; it will separate from the margin marker.

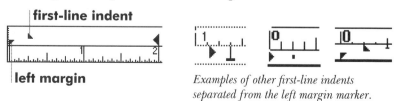

Examples of other first-line indents separated from the left margin marker.

Most programs have default tabs set about every half inch. As soon as you set a tab anywhere in the ruler, all the defaults to the left of that point disappear; they are still present and available to the right.

A good program typically has at least four different sorts of tabs. Their actual appearance may vary, as shown below, but they all act the same.

- **Left-aligned tab:** if you press the Tab key and get to a left-aligned tab, the text lines up at the tab stop and types out to the right, so the *left* side of the text is aligned.

    Typically the marker has a little tail pointing to the right, in the direction the text will type.

    This text
    is set with
    a left-aligned
    tab.

- **Right-aligned tab:** if you press the Tab key and get to a right-aligned tab, the text lines up at the tab stop and types out to the left, so the *right* side of the text is aligned. It actually looks like it's typing backwards.

    Typically the marker has a little tail pointing to the left, in the direction the text will type.

    This is the tab to use for columns of numbers, to keep all the ones and tens and so on in their proper column. Also, if you want to send the date over to the right side, set a right-aligned tab directly on the right margin.

    | | This text | 493 |
    | | is set with a | 5 |
    | | right-aligned | 1,094,320 |
    | | tab. It's especially | 5,672 |
    | | good with numbers. | |

- **Centered tab:** if you press the Tab key and get to a centered tab, the text *centers* itself under the tab. As you type, the text actually moves out in both directions. Typically the marker has no tail at all.

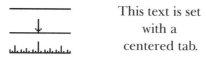

> This text is set
> with a
> centered tab.

- **Decimal tab:** if you press the Tab key and get to a decimal tab, the text aligns itself at the decimal place or period. As you type, the text moves out to the left; as soon as you hit the period or decimal, any characters following it will move out to the right.

  This is the tab to use for keeping dollars and cents in their proper columns, to keep the decimal point lined up when you have a varying amount of numbers following it, and to create the numbered paragraphs as shown on the following pages.

  Typically the marker has no tail, but a little dot next to it.

1. This number was set to a decimal tab.
2. There is also a tab to start the text.

45.9
123,453.0056
.53
1.02

Here are the first-line indent and tab set-ups for several common ways of arranging numbered blocks of text.

1. This is the way text will align if you don't set any tabs at all. You type the number, a period, a space, then the text.

2. This is the same as above, but the text starts with a tab. Tabs are important on the Mac because spaces are not always the same, so characters don't align very well without them.

tab

first-line indent

tab

3. Now, to create this example, set the first-line indent at the far left. Set the margin marker where the text should align.

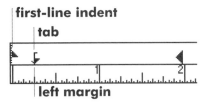

left margin

4. When you hit the **Return** key, the insertion point will return to the **first-line indent**; as it *word wraps*, it comes back to the *left margin marker*.

5. Also set a tab directly on the margin marker. This allows you to tab over *to the first word of the text* so that word aligns with the rest of the word-wrapped lines.

6. If you don't set a tab at that margin marker, the text will look like this paragraph, where the first word is not aligned with the rest of the text.

no tab

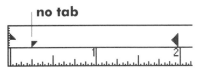

7. Now, that hanging paragraph works very well—it keeps everything nice and neat. A problem arises when the numbers get past ten. Have you ever noticed this happen:

    8. Text.
    9. More text.
    10. Uh oh—notice the periods and the text—they are no longer aligned! That extra digit in the 10 bumped everything over.

8. How to solve that? Well, your first-line indent should be *all* the way to the left.

9. Since the numbers have a period after them, you can set a decimal tab in far enough from the left edge to allow space for the largest number you will have. If you have no decimal tab available or you're not using a period, set a right-aligned tab; it'll do the same thing.

decimal tab (or use a right-aligned tab)

10. Set your left margin marker where you want all the text to align.

11. Set a left-aligned tab directly on the margin marker.

12. Now, you have to do this: To type your first number, from the far left hit the Tab key; this will take you to the decimal/right-aligned tab where you type your number; the number will line up on the right.

    Now hit the Tab again to take you to the first line of your text; as you input the text, it will word wrap back to where you set your left margin.

    When you hit the Return key, the insertion point will go back to the far left where the first-line indent is, and you can begin again.

Widows & Orphans.

Never leave widows and orphans
bereft on the page.

Now obviously this term isn't referring to bereaved widows and orphans such as some of us are ourselves—no, these are actually long-standing technical, typographic terms.

When a paragraph ends and leaves fewer than seven characters (not words, characters) on the last line, that last line is called a **widow**. Worse than leaving one word there is leaving part of a word, the other part being hyphenated on the line above.

A gentle joyousness—a mighty mildness of repose in swiftness, invested the gliding whale. Not the white bull Jupiter swimming away with ravished Europa clinging to his graceful horns; his lovely, leering eyes sideways intent upon the maid; with smooth bewitching fleetness, rippling straight for the nuptial bower in Crete; not Jove, not that great majesty Supreme! did surpass the glorified White Whale as he so divinely swam. **widow**

On each soft side— coincident with the parted swell, that but once leaving him, then flowed so wide away— on each bright side, the whale shed off en- ticings. **an even worse widow**

When the last line of a paragraph, be it ever so long, won't fit at the bottom of a column and must end itself at the top of the next column, that is an **orphan.**

...Moby Dick moved on, still withholding from sight the full terrors of his submerged trunk, entirely hiding the wrenched hideousness of his jaw. But soon the fore part of him slowly rose from the water; for an instant his whole marbleized body formed a high arch, like Virginia's Natural Bridge, and warningly waving his bannered flukes in the air, the grand god revealed himself, sounded, and went out of sight. Hoveringly halting, and dipping on the wing, the white sea-fowls longingly lingered over the agitated pool

orphan

that he left.

With oars apeak, and paddles down, the sheets of their sails adrift, the three boats now stilly floated, awaiting Moby Dick's appearance.

In long Indian file, as when herons take wing, the white birds were now all flying towards Ahab's boat; and when within a few yards began fluttering over the water there, wheeling round and round, with joyous, expectant cries.

Herman Melville, *Moby Dick*

Avoid both of these circumstances. Sometimes you'll need to rewrite copy, or at least add or delete a word or two. Sometimes you'll have to take spacing out of the letters, words, or lines, depending on the program you're working in. Sometimes widening a margin just a hair will do it. But it must be done. Widows and orphans on a page are tacky.

See what I mean?

H yphenations & line breaks.

Avoid more than two hyphenations in a row.
Avoid too many hyphenations in any paragraph.
Avoid stupid hyphenations.
Never hyphenate a heading.
Break lines sensibly.

It's amazing how often silly line breaks show up. A line break is simply that—where a heading or sentence breaks off at the end of a line.

This is more often critical in headings or in short blocks of text than in long manuscripts, although even in lengthy text you can find those classic cases, like hyphenating the word *therapist* so it becomes *the-rapist*. We've all seen strange hyphenations like turn-ed, or-phans, occuren-ce. Some, obviously, are downright wrong. Not only are they wrong, they're a gross sign of unprofessionalism. Watch them. Don't rely on your software package to do it the best way. Use a dictionary to verify any word that looks a bit odd. Read the lines carefully; even if a word is broken properly, pick up on any instances where there may be a split second of confusion, ambiguity, racism, sexism, stupidity, etc., resulting from breaking the line at that particular point. If there is, fix it. Notice how awkward these sentences are (these actually came back from a typesetter):

> **SRJC is an open-access cam-**
> **pus.**

> **Any prospective or interested stud-**
> **ent can contact the Instructional Office.**

Almost as bad as dumb hyphenations are too many hyphenations in a row. Sometimes you can't avoid hyphenating, but it's never necessary to hyphenate three times in a row, or six of the eight lines in a paragraph. In those cases, you really must adjust something.

Often, too many hyphenations are the result of using a justified alignment (text aligned on both sides of the column, as this is) on a line that is too short for the point size. If you can't possibly left-align the text, try rewording, adjusting letter or word spacing if that's possible, kerning (see page 33), widening the margin, or adding spaces before the offending word on a justified line to bump it down to the next line.

Never hyphenate a word in a headline

Any headline can be broken at a logical point. Even though you may have no hyphenations in a headline, insensitive line breaks can still make your text awkward or ambiguous. Generally, group lines of a heading into appropriate grammatical sections. Which of the following would be more appropriate?:

Jimmy's Lemonade Stand	**Jimmy's Lemonade Stand**
Parade in the Bay Area was a Success	**Parade in the Bay Area was a Success**
The Theater presents Don Quixote de la Mancha	**The Theater presents Don Quixote de la Mancha**

Watch line breaks in body text as well

Most of the text you create is flush left with a ragged right margin. Try to keep the right margin as even as possible, for the visual effect as well as for smoother reading—it can be bothersome to have lines ending at radically different points. This means you may need to bump words from one line down to the next line, or occasionally rewrite copy to adjust the lines.

Few things are pure, and they are seldom simple; and of all the impure and unsimple things in this world which befog and bedevil the minds of men, their ideas about women deserve to take first place.
—Oscar Wilde

Few things are pure, and they are seldom simple; and of all the impure and unsimple things in this world which befog and bedevil the minds of men, their ideas about women deserve to take first place.
—Oscar Wilde

Simply bumping the word 'and' from the first line to the second (by inserting a couple of spaces before the word) rearranged all the following lines to give a smoother right margin. Then I also aligned *Oscar Wilde*.

Leading, or linespace.

Keep the linespacing consistent.

Linespacing within a paragraph should be consistent. We often set an initial cap or a word in a larger point size than the rest of the text. This affects the linespacing, or leading (the space between the lines of type); if even one letter or word is larger, the linespacing adjusts to fit the larger character(s), creating uneven spacing.

The history of the term leading (pronounced *ledding*) may give you a better grasp of what leading itself accomplishes and how you can best adjust it.

Until the early '70s (yes, the 1970s), all printed type was set in hot metal. Each letter—each and every little letter—was cast onto a tiny piece of lead *backwards* so when printed the letter would be facing the right direction. All these letters were lined up in a row, with other tiny pieces of blank metal stuck between the words to separate them. Even the newer linotype machines (which composed these little pieces of type whole lines at a time instead of one letter at a time) used the same principle. Between each line of type another piece of blank lead was inserted to separate the lines—this was called the *leading*.

Now, the type was measured in points, just like the type on the Mac (72 points per inch). The leading was also measured in points. If the type was **10** points high and the little piece of lead inserted between the lines was **2** points high, then the **2** points was *added onto* the point size of the type and the leading was called **12** point. Got that?

10 point type on
2 points of linespace —— *a piece of lead 2 points thick*
makes 12 pt. leading

Typically, a standard unit of measure for the leading between the lines is 20 percent of the point size: in the example on the previous page, the type is 10 point, the leading would be 12 point. (Many manuals for Macintosh programs call the percentage 120 percent, which is the same as adding on the 20 percent.)

What all this boils down to is that when you type on the Mac, you automatically get a 20 percent leading (that's **auto leading**). When a word or character is made larger, it automatically comes with more leading. This creates an awkward look to a paragraph, as then one line has more space after it than the others. For instance, if you use 12-point type, the auto leading is around 14 (about 120% of the point size). But when you insert a 24-point initial letter into your paragraph, the leading for that one line automatically bumps up to about 29.

In this example,
the first letter is larger and
disrupts the even linespacing
of the rest of the paragraph.

This paragraph
also has a large initial cap,
but the leading has been
adjusted.

It's usually possible to correct the line spacing, depending on the program you're creating it in.

- If your application allows you to adjust the leading, then select the entire paragraph and reset the leading to what it originally was for the *smaller* type.

- Sometimes you can adjust the leading, but it won't let you go smaller than the auto-leading for the larger size, the one that's disruptive; in that case you'll need to adjust the line spacing for the entire paragraph to match the *larger* size.

- If you're having difficulty fixing the leading in a page layout program, you may find it easier to set the initial cap in its own text block and move it in next to the rest of the text as a separate unit.

- In some of the less sophisticated programs, you can't adjust the line spacing at all. But you can sneak this trick in: select one of the blank spaces between the words on a line; change the point size of the blank space to the same size as the large initial cap or word that's causing all this trouble. You'll have to do this separately for each line in the paragraph in order to make them all match.

Adjust leading with all caps

You'll find extra, awkward leading between lines of all capital letters (on those rare occasions when you use all caps!). That's because caps have no "descenders"—those parts of the lowercase letters g, j, p, q, and y that drop below the rest of the letters. To tighten up the leading, figure out what the auto leading is (120% of the point size). Then set the leading to less than that. For instance, the auto leading for 36-point type would be about 43; reset it for less than 43. Usually on all caps you can actually reduce it to less than the number of the point size of the type; e.g., 36-point type and 34-point leading—try it! Notice that the example below is 18-point type with 16 leading, or linespace.

TOO MUCH LINESPACE

(18-point type; Auto leading)

LINESPACING ADJUSTED

(18-point type; 16-point leading)

The same is true of a line, generally a headline, that has few descenders. Lacking descenders, lines with no visual interruption in them can create space that looks larger than necessary.

Too much spacing

(18-point type; Auto leading)

Better spacing

(18-point type; 16-point leading)

Adjust the spacing between paragraphs

To have more space between paragraphs on a typewriter, our only option was to hit the carriage return twice. You've probably noticed in Macintosh typesetting that this turns out to be an excessive amount, giving a clunky look to your paragraphs. Most software applications that use type, such as word processing or page layout programs, have a means for you to separate paragraphs by as few points as you would like. Generally it is found in a "Paragraph" command.

Wherever you find this feature in the particular application you are using, you can add a few points in a box usually called **after.** These few points *after* mean that whenever you press Return, those few points will be *added onto* the leading used in the previous paragraph before going on to the next paragraph. If you are using 10-point type with 12-point leading, you can add 5 points after, creating about half a linespace between paragraphs. The text you are reading here is set 10/13 with 6 extra points between the paragraphs.

It is redundant to indent the first line of paragraphs if you are setting extra space between them. Use one or the other. But do always use *something*, or the text becomes difficult to read.

Justified text.

Justify text only if the line is long enough to prevent awkward and inconsistent word spacing.

The power of a word processor is so much fun that it's easy to go overboard. The tendency is to try to do all those things we couldn't do on a typewriter, and one of the most common things is to justify all the text (that is, to align it on both margins, like this paragraph). On a few kinds of typewriters it was possible to do this with a great deal of trouble, and heaven forbid if you made a typo and had to go back later and correct it. But with these magic machines, a push of a button and the entire body of text aligns itself. It's irresistible.

Resist it. The only time you can safely get away with justifying text is if your type is small enough and your line is long enough, as in books where the text goes all the way across the page. If your line is shorter, or if you don't have many words on the line, then as the type aligns to the margins the words space themselves to accommodate it. It usually looks awkward. You've seen newspaper columns where all text is justified, often with a word stretching all the way across the column, or a little word on either side of the column with a big gap in the middle. Gross. But that's what can happen with justified type. When you do it, the effect might not be as radical as the newspaper column, but if your lines are relatively short, you will inevitably end up with uncomfortable gaps between some words, with other words looking all squished together:

"A traveller! By my faith, you have great reason to be sad: I fear you have sold your own lands to see other men's; then, to have seen much and to have nothing, is to have rich eyes and poor hands."

Rosalind
W. Shakespeare

— When the space between the words becomes greater than the space between the lines, it creates what are called "rivers" running through the type.

When your work comes out of the printer, turn it upside down and squint at it. The rivers will be very easy to spot. Get rid of them. Try squinting at the example on the previous page.

Here is a general guideline for determining if your line length is long enough to satisfactorily justify the text: the line length in picas should be about twice the point size of the type; that is, if the type you are using is 12 point, the line length should be about 24 picas (24 picas is 4 inches—simply multiply the number of inches by 6, as there are 6 picas per inch).

Justified text was the style for many years—we grew up on it. But there has been a great deal of research on readability (how easy something is to read) and it shows that those disruptive, inconsistent gaps between the words inhibit the flow of reading. Besides, they look dumb. Keep your eyes open as you look at professionally-printed work (magazines, newsletters, annual reports, journals) and you'll find there's a very strong trend now to align type on the left and leave the right ragged.

Isn't that an odd thing to read as you see this whole book justified? But it's just like the choice to use all caps: when you choose to justify type, you must realize you are choosing that *look* and sacrificing the most effective word spacing. Depending on the project, one may be more important than the other. For this book, I wanted the *look* of the justified line and I felt the line length was long enough to give me a minimum amount of awkward word spacing (although I must admit I still find the uneven word spacing irritating, even on this length of line; I can't have everything, they tell me).

Hanging the punctuation.

Hang punctuation off the aligned edge to eliminate any visual interruption of the text.

Hanging the punctuation is particularly important in larger sizes of text, such as headlines, or in quoted material, no matter what its size. The easiest way to explain the concept is by example:

> **"When I get a little money,
> I buy books.
> If there is any left over,
> I buy food and clothes."**
>
> *Desiderius Erasmus*

Notice how the quotation mark visually interrupts the left alignment. The first line appears to be indented rather than flush left.

> **"When I get a little money,
> I buy books.
> If there is any left over,
> I buy food and clothes."**
>
> *Desiderius Erasmus*

The block of text above has been adjusted to keep the left alignment visually intact—the quotation mark has been *hung*.

> **Thou art thy mother's glass
> and she in thee
> Calls back the lovely April
> of her prime.**
>
> *William Shakespeare*

Notice above how even something as small as a period can create a visual misalignment.

**Thou art thy mother's glass
and she in thee
Calls back the lovely April
of her prime.**

William Shakespeare

Hanging the period preserves the strength of the alignment.

Squint at any text that has a strong flush alignment and notice where the alignment is broken with punctuation. Look at hyphens, periods, commas, single or double quotation marks, bullets—anything that creates a slight break in the visual continuity. Then hang it.

Different software applications deal with this in different ways. In some applications it's just not possible, as in most word processing programs. You will need to check with the manual for your particular program.

Inserting *non-breaking spaces* is one way to hang punctuation in a short block of text. Both of the examples in this chapter were adjusted that way. In the first example, after the type was set and the distraction noticed, I inserted an *em space* at the beginning of each line. An em space is like an em dash—it takes up a space about the size of a capital letter M in that font and size (see page 19 for information on hyphens and dashes).

In the second example, I inserted a *thin space* at the end of each of the first three lines, and added two thins after the by-line, since the by-line is a smaller point size (ens, ems, and thins are proportional to the size of type). A thin space takes up about one-fourth the amount of room as an em space.

Some applications allow you to pick up the letters and marks, one by one, and place them wherever you like. Occasionally it may be easiest to set the offending line in a block of its own and manually hang the entire line. Whichever method you use, hanging the punctuation is obviously one of the last touches of detailing to do in a document. But it really must be done.

Serif and sans serif.

Serif type is more readable and is best for text; sans serif type is more legible and is best used for headlines.

Type can generally be classified into two major groups: serif and sans serif. Those little ditties at the ends of the strokes of the letter are serifs. If a font doesn't have those, it's called "sans serif," because "sans" means "without."

Readability

Many studies have shown that serif type is more *readable* in extended text than sans serif. It's not clear exactly why; suggestions are that the serifs tend to lead the eye along the horizontal line, or that the thick/thin variations in the strokes of most serif type eases reading, or perhaps simply the fact that we all grew up learning to read from books that used serif type. Whatever the reason, it has been well-established that serif type is easier to read, particularly in extended text. Have you ever seen a novel printed in sans serif type?

Legibility

Sans serif, on the other hand, has been shown to be more *legible*. What's the difference? Well, legibility refers more to character recognition than to reading blocks of text. Put in practical terms, sans serif is easier to recognize at a glance for short little bursts of type, such as in headlines on a page or in a signage system in corporate headquarters. A full page set in sans serif may initially *appear* to be easier to read, but in the long run it proves not to be.

General use

Notice in publications how serif and sans serif fonts are used. Very typically you'll find that headlines are set in sans serif and the main body of text is set in serif. That's because it's a time-tested and infinitely variable solution.

Sans serif in text

If you do insist on setting your body text in a sans serif, keep these things in mind to improve its readability:

- Use a shorter line length (see page 52 regarding line length).
- Set not more than seven or eight words on the line (serif type can handle ten to twelve words).
- Avoid manipulating the type style to make it even less readable; i.e., as few bold or italic or outlined or shadowed words as possible.

Examples

Read this paragraph and the following one while trying to be particularly sensitive to which one feels a touch easier to read. Remember, *readability* becomes more important in lengthy text, such as a book or thesis paper, rather than in a paragraph or two of advertisement copy, but you can probably get a sense for it even in these short blocks.

When the term *legibility* is discussed, it's referring to display type, such as headlines or signs. Read the following headlines, noticing which one is more distinguishable at a quick glance. Of course, you can *read* both of them, but once you become aware of the subtle differences in readability and legibility, you begin to have a clue as to how important the selection of a particular typeface can be to effective communication.

For Sale For Sale

Combining typefaces.

Unless you have a background in design and typography, never combine more than two typefaces on the same page.

Never combine two serif fonts on the same page, and never combine two sans serif fonts on the same page.

When all those typefaces are staring at you from the Font menu and all it takes is a click of the mouse to change from one to the other, it's hard to keep yourself under control and not make the page look like a ransom note. Try.

You can't go too wrong if you keep it down to two typefaces in a document. A particularly good combination is to use a sans serif for headings and a serif for the body copy (see the previous chapter). Now, within each typeface, it's fine to make some of it bold or italic or playful occasionally (try to keep the style you choose consistent with the purpose and meaning of the text).

But you should never (unless you've had design and typography training and really know what you're doing) combine two sans serif typefaces on the same page, like Avant Garde and Helvetica. Without going into a lot of design theory, the basic principle is that there is not enough contrast between the faces—they are too similar to each other and set up a subtle conflict. The combination will make your page look tacky, unprofessional, and dumb.

Combining two serif typefaces can be done more easily, but again, it takes some training to understand how to do it effectively.

If you have no background in design or typography, then it is very safe to stick to two typefaces, one serif and one sans serif. Even though you may be saying to yourself right now, "I'm not designing anything anyway," you are. Every time you turn on your Macintosh and create a document to be printed, you're designing the page that's going to come out. If it's a newsletter, a poster, an ad, a thesis paper, an essay, or even a letter to Grandma, you are designing that page. And there's no reason on earth not to make that page look good.

Helvetica and Avant Garde do not have enough contrast between them to look good together on one page. Notice the subtle differences in the shapes of the letters: Avant Garde is very geometric, while Helvetica has more classic shapes.

Helvetica

This creates a situation where there is neither *concord*, where all elements are working together, nor is there *contrast*, where elements are set up intentionally to contrast and strengthen each other. What results is *conflict*.

Avant Garde

Notice how the two sans serifs above compete with each other—they have some similarities and some differences, but not enough of either to work effectively together.

Strengthen the contrasts
When combining typefaces, don't be a wimp. Contrast with strength. If one face is light and airy, choose a dense black one to go with it. If one face is small, make the other one large. If you set one all caps, set the other lowercase.

Avoid weak contrasts, such as a semi-bold type with a bold type; avoid combining a script with an italic; or combining large type with almost-as-large type. Put some chutzpa into it!

M iscellaneous.

Just a few asides that are important but don't rate their own little chapters.

- Use italic and bold as you would a rich dessert—they're fine occasionally, but easy to overdose on.

- The traditional, standard format for A.M. and P.M. is *small caps*, which we couldn't do on a typewriter so we were taught to type them all caps. When set in all caps, though, the letters are very large and attach too much importance to themselves. Now we have the means to set them properly: type the letters in *lowercase;* select them; choose "Small Caps" from your style menu—virtually every application that uses type has this option. (Small caps turns *lowercase* letters into capital letters that are not much bigger than lowercase itself.) There should be a space after the number and periods after the letters: 8:35 A.M.

- Regarding punctuation and parentheses, remember that the sentence punctuation goes *after* the closing parenthesis if what is inside the parentheses is part of the sentence (as this phrase here). That goes for commas, semi-colons, and colons also.

 If what is inside the parentheses is an entire statement of its own, the ending punctuation should be inside also, as in the paragraph above regarding small caps.

- When placing more than one column of text on a page, be sure to align the first *baselines* of each column. The baseline is the invisible line the type sits on, and when two bodies of text are next to each other, it is critical that the first lines across the columns align.

- Don't be afraid of "white space"! (It's called white, even if the paper is black; it just means the space where there is no element printed on the page.) The area on the page that does not have text or graphics on it is just as important as the area that does. You may not be conscious of it yet, but your eyes are aware of it and how it's affecting everything else on the page. Don't be afraid to have wide margins, empty space before or after a major heading, a short bit of copy tucked up in the upper left instead of spread out in the middle of the page. That's one of the greatest differences between a clean, professional, sophisticated look and an amateur look—the professional is not afraid to leave plenty of white space!

- When placing text inside a box, don't crowd it. Leave plenty of room on all sides. Generally the ideal is to have the same amount of space on all four sides, visually. If you are leaving more space on one or two sides intentionally, then make it obvious.

> **This text is crowded,
> thus making it
> unappealing to read.**

> **This text has more
> breathing space,
> thus becoming more
> readable and inviting.**

- When typing numbers, never use the lowercase L (l) for the number one (1), nor the capital letter O for a zero (0). Besides the fact that they have different shapes, Mac reacts to them differently; if you'll be doing any sort of calculating, Mac will get very confused if an L is found in a list of numbers.

- Make a conscious effort to be consistent. If a heading is aligned left, then align left all the headings. If a heading is 18-point bold, then make all the headings 18-point bold. If a page number is on the bottom outer margin, they should all be there. Etc. etc. etc. Look for consistency in tabs, indents, fonts, punctuation, alignments, margins on all sides, etc.

- When listing items, as in a résumé or contents box, use a bullet of some sort rather than the hyphen or asterisk. The hyphen and asterisk were fine on the typewriter when we had no other option, but now we can use the standard bullet • (Option 8), or any of a great variety of others: ❧ ❤ ❑ ☛ ■ (these come from the font Zapf Dingbats).

- Avoid abbreviating whenever possible. Rarely is it necessary to abbreviate St. for Street or Dr. for Drive. In body text, avoid words like lbs. for pounds or oz. for ounces (something like an order form, of course, is different).

  When possible, spell out the name of the state as well. If you are going to abbreviate it, then at least do it right: states are now all abbreviated with two capital letters and no periods. California should never be abbreviated as Ca, Ca., or Calif. It looks uneducated, or at least old-fashioned.

- In headlines, the punctuation often appears unnecessarily large, placing too much visual emphasis on itself. Commas, apostrophes, quotation marks, periods, etc., should all be reduced a point size or two.

"Everything must end; meanwhile we must amuse ourselves."

—*Voltaire*

12-point text; no adjustments made

"Everything must end; meanwhile we must amuse ourselves."

—*Voltaire*

12-point text; 10-point quotes and punctuation; punctuation hung

- When selecting a word to change into italic, be sure to select the space *before* the word, as well as the word itself; don't select the space *after* the word. Italic fonts take up less space than roman (non-italic) fonts. This, in addition to the fact that they slant to the right, can sometimes create a distracting bit of extra space before the italic word unless you also italicize that space and thus make it smaller. Yes, it's subtle.

- On a typewriter we were taught that a paragraph indent should be five spaces, so we would always set a tab for that paragaraph indent accordingly. Now we can set a first-line indent, right? But the size of that five-space indent is no longer appropriate with the professional, proportional type we are now using—it is a bit large and clunky-looking.

Traditional typesetting standards set a paragraph indent of **one em** (a space equal to the point size of the type being used; that is, in 12-point type an em space is 12 points wide). Visually, this is roughly equivalent to two spaces, or the width of a capital letter M. If your program does not allow you to specify points for indents, just use a sensitive approximation.

Really, this is true—check the paragraph indents in any book on your shelf (except a computer book produced within the last five years).

Quiz.

In the following text there are over a dozen mistakes that need editing. They may be typos, inconsistencies, bad line breaks, wrong hyphenations, widows or orphans, or any of the myriad items mentioned in this little book. See how many changes you can suggest for making the piece look more professional. A few suggestions are on the following pages.

The Solace of Tra-vel

To the untravelled, territory other than their own familiar heath is invariably *fascinating*. Next to *love*, it is the one thing which *solaces* and *delights*. Things new are too *important* to be neglected, and *mind*, which is a mere refection of *sensory impressions*, succumbs to the *flood* of objects. Thus lovers are *forgotten*, *sorrows* laid aside, *death* hidden from view. There is a *world* of accumulated feeling back of the trite dramatic *expression* -- "I am going *away*".

THEODORE DREISER

Sister Carrie

• Wimpy contrast of fonts

needs kerning

The Solace of Tra-vel

wrong and bad line break

underline is too close and too heavy

needs kerning

To the untravelled, territory other than their own familiar heath is invariably *fascinating.* Next to love, it is the one thing which *solaces* and *delights.* Things new are too *important* to be neglected, and *mind*, which is a mere refection of *sensory impressions,* succumbs to the *flood* of objects. Thus lovers are *forgotten, sorrows* laid aside, *death* hidden from view. There is a *world* of accumulated feeling back of the trite dramatic *expression* — "I am going away."

wrong fonts

line spacing is inconsistent

too much space after period

misspelled word

period belongs inside quote marks

wrong quote marks

should be an emdash with no spaces

THEODORE DREISER

unnecessary to have this set in all caps; makes it too important

widow

Sister Carrie

avoid underlining; besides, it is redundant to underline and *italicize*

these two items need a stronger visual connection with each other; they are also too large for their purpose

• too many word italicized

• too many hyphenated lines

• too many different sans serifs on one page

• lack of contrast or concord

• line length is too short for justified text

Possible alternative.

This is but one of a myriad of possibilities for setting this prose.

The Solace of Travel

To the untravelled, territory
other than their own familiar
heath is invariably fascinating.
Next to love, it is the one thing
which solaces and delights.
Things new are too important
to be neglected, and mind,
which is a mere reflection of
sensory impressions, succumbs to
the flood of objects. Thus lovers
are forgotten, sorrows laid aside,
death hidden from view. There
is a world of accumulated feeling
back of the trite dramatic
expression—"I am going away."

Theodore Dreiser
Sister Carrie

You know my methods. Use them.

— Sir Arthur Conan Doyle

Appendix A. ∎

The following is a compendium of the rules established in this book. You might want to check through them each time you complete a publication.

❏ Use only one space between sentences.

❏ Use real quotation marks.

❏ Check the punctuation used with quote marks.

❏ Use real apostrophes.

❏ Make sure the apostrophes are where they belong.

❏ Use en and em dashes where appropriate.

❏ Use the special characters whenever necessary, including super- and subscript.

❏ Spend the time to create nice fractions.

❏ If a correctly-spelled word needs an accent mark, use it.

❏ Don't underline.

❏ Never use all caps in body text; rarely use it in heads.

❏ Kern all headlines where necessary.

❏ If printing to the LaserWriter, never use a city-named font.

❏ Never use the space bar to align text.

❏ Use a one-em first-line indent on all indented paragraphs.

❏ Use a decimal or right-aligned tab for the numbers in numbered paragraphs.

❏ Leave no widows or orphans.

❏ Never have more than two hyphenations in a row.

❏ Avoid too many hyphenations in any paragraph.

❏ On every line of text in the document, watch all line breaks carefully. Be sensible.

❏ Keep the line spacing consistent.

❏ Tighten up the leading in lines with all caps or with few ascenders and descenders.

❏ Adjust the spacing between paragraphs; rarely use a full line of space between paragraphs in body text.

❏ Either indent the first line of paragraphs or add extra space between them— not both.

❏ Never justify the text on a short line.

❏ Hang the punctuation off the aligned edge.

❏ Use serif type for body text unless you are going to compensate for the lower readability of sans serif.

❏ Never combine two serif fonts on one page.

❏ Never combine two san serif fonts on one page.

❏ Never combine more than two typefaces on one page (unless you've studied typography). So the gist is: if you're going to use more than one face, use one serif and one sans serif.

❏ Don't be a wimp.

❏ Use italic and bold sparingly.

❏ Use proper punctuation with parentheses.

❏ Align the first baselines of juxtaposed columns.

❏ Encourage white space.

❏ Don't crowd text inside a box—let it breathe.

❏ Be consistent.

❏ Use some sort of bullet when listing items, not a hyphen.

❏ Avoid abbreviations.

❏ Use small caps for A.M. and P.M.; space once after the number, and use periods.

❏ Reduce the size of the punctuation marks in headlines.

❏ Set the space *before* an italic word also in italic.

Appendix B.

■

The following is a list of the most often-used
special characters and accent marks.

"	Option [	opening double quote
"	Option Shift [	closing double quote
'	Option]	opening single quote
'	Option Shift]	closing single quote; apostrophe
–	Option hyphen	en dash
—	Option Shift hyphen	em dash
…	Option ;	ellipsis (this character can't be separated at the end of a line as three periods can)
•	Option 8	bullet (easy to remember as it's the asterisk key)
■	n (*Zapf Dingbats*)	black ballot box
□	n (*Zapf Dingbats, outlined*)	empty ballot box
fi	Option Shift 5	ligature of f and i
fl	Option Shift 6	ligature of f and l
©	Option g	
™	Option 2	
®	Option r	
°	Option Shift 8	degree symbol (e.g., 102°F)
¢	Option $	
/	Option Shift !	fraction bar (this doesn't descend below the line as the slash does)
¡	Option 1	
¿	Option Shift ?	
£	Option 3	
ç	Option c	
Ç	Option Shift c	— continued

Remember, on the accent marks over the letters, press the Option key with the letter, then press the letter you want under it (see page 27).

´   Option e

`   Option ~   (upper left or next to the spacebar)

¨   Option u

~   Option n

^   Option i

Index.

■

This book was produced on a Mac SE using the software applications MacWrite II and Aldus Pagemaker. All graphic images were screen dumps cleaned up in SuperPaint. Proof prints were made on the LaserWriter; final output on a Linotronic 300.

Main type families used are Futura and Baskerville. All fonts in this edition are from Bitstream, Inc.

Design and production by the author.

About the author.

Robin Williams is a part-time instructor at Santa Rosa Junior College in Santa Rosa, California. After many years of teaching graphic design and typography and coordinating the Design Graphics Program, she discovered the Macintosh. It didn't take long to switch from t-squares-and-triangles-and-rubber-cement-and-rubylith-all-over-the-place graphics to turn-off-the-switch-and-the-mess-is-all-cleaned-up graphics. Robin now teaches desktop design, electronic typesetting, and related Macintosh courses at the college and in the training department at ComputerLand. She also offers private training for individuals and businesses.

Robin has written other books, including *The Little Mac Book, PageMaker 4: An Easy Desk Reference,* and *The PC is not a typewriter,* all published by Peachpit Press.